I0815330

Dirty Work

# DIRTY COMMUNITY JOBS

Kenny Abdo

Fly!
An Imprint of Abdo Zoom
abdobooks.com

**abdobooks.com**

Published by Abdo Zoom, a division of ABDO, P.O. Box 398166, Minneapolis, Minnesota 55439. 

Printed in the United States of America, North Mankato, Minnesota.
052025
092025

Photo Credits: AdobeStock, Alamy, Shutterstock
Production Contributors: Kenny Abdo, Jennie Forsberg, Grace Hansen
Design Contributors: Candice Keimig, Neil Klinepier, Colleen McLaren

**Library of Congress Control Number: 2024947691**

**Publisher's Cataloging-in-Publication Data**

Names: Abdo, Kenny, author.
Title: Dirty community jobs / by Kenny Abdo
Description: Minneapolis, Minnesota : Abdo Zoom, 2026 | Series: Dirty work | Includes online resources and index.
Identifiers: ISBN 9781098288709 (lib. bdg.) | ISBN 9781098289409 (ebook) | ISBN 9781098289751 (Read-to-me ebook)
Subjects: LCSH: Sanitation--Juvenile literature. | Careers--Juvenile literature. | Community organization--Juvenile literature. | Employees--Health and hygiene--Juvenile literature. | Refuse and refuse disposal--Juvenile literature.
Classification: DDC 331.70--dc23

# TABLE OF CONTENTS

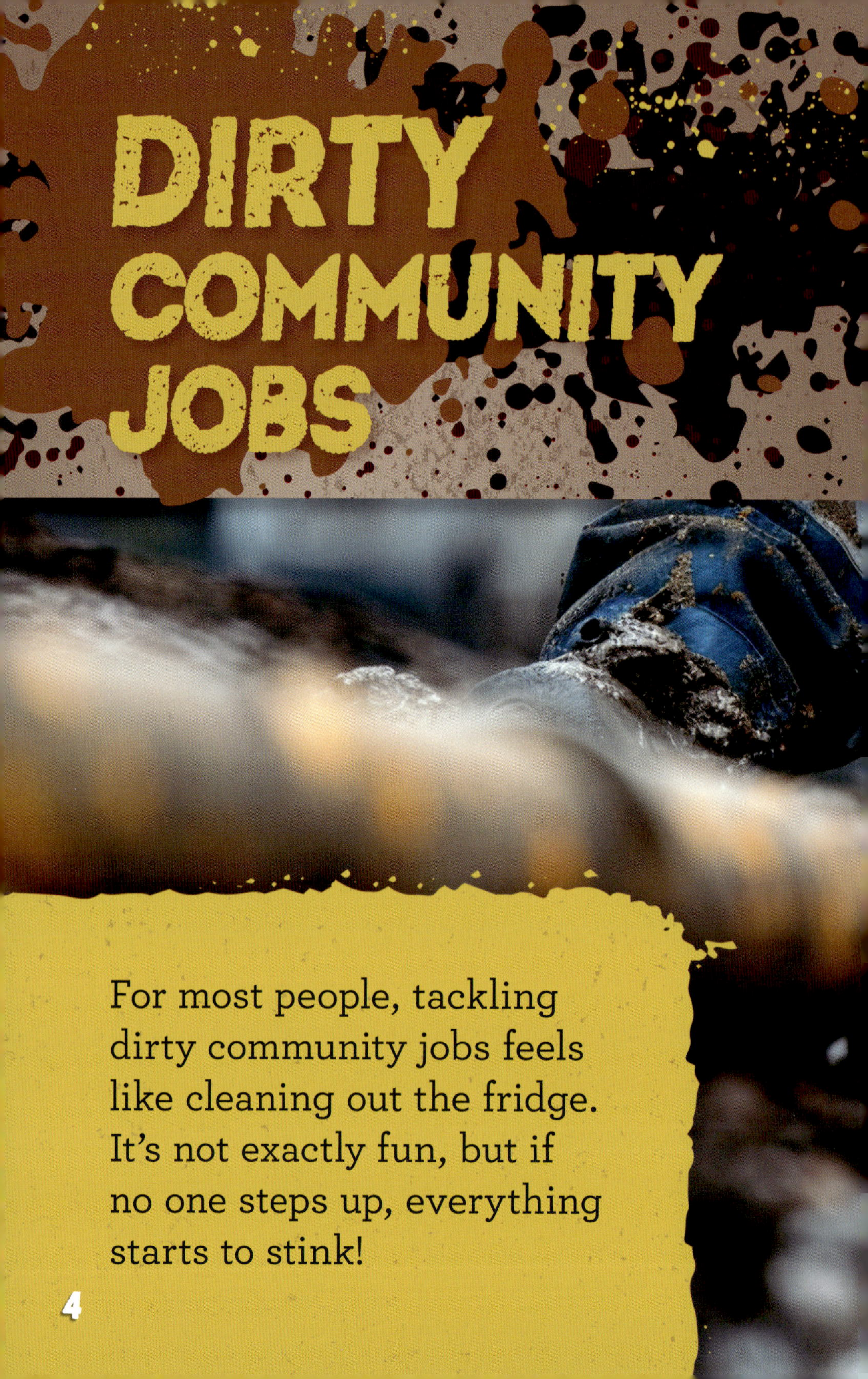

# DIRTY COMMUNITY JOBS

For most people, tackling dirty community jobs feels like cleaning out the fridge. It's not exactly fun, but if no one steps up, everything starts to stink!

# THE DIRT

Community workers promote public health and social **welfare**. Caregivers, social workers, and community health workers support those in need.

However, there are messier community jobs. These important jobs usually deal with stomach-turning waste, illness, and toxic materials. The work puts the *ewww* in community!

# THE WORK

**Grease trap** cleaners help remove the thick, foul-smelling sludge from restaurants. This prevents plumbing issues and maintains cleanliness. To most, it is one slick job!

**Sewage treatment** plants process and treat wastewater. They make sure it is clean before it is released back into the environment. The operators often work with **raw** sewage, sludge, and unpleasant odors.

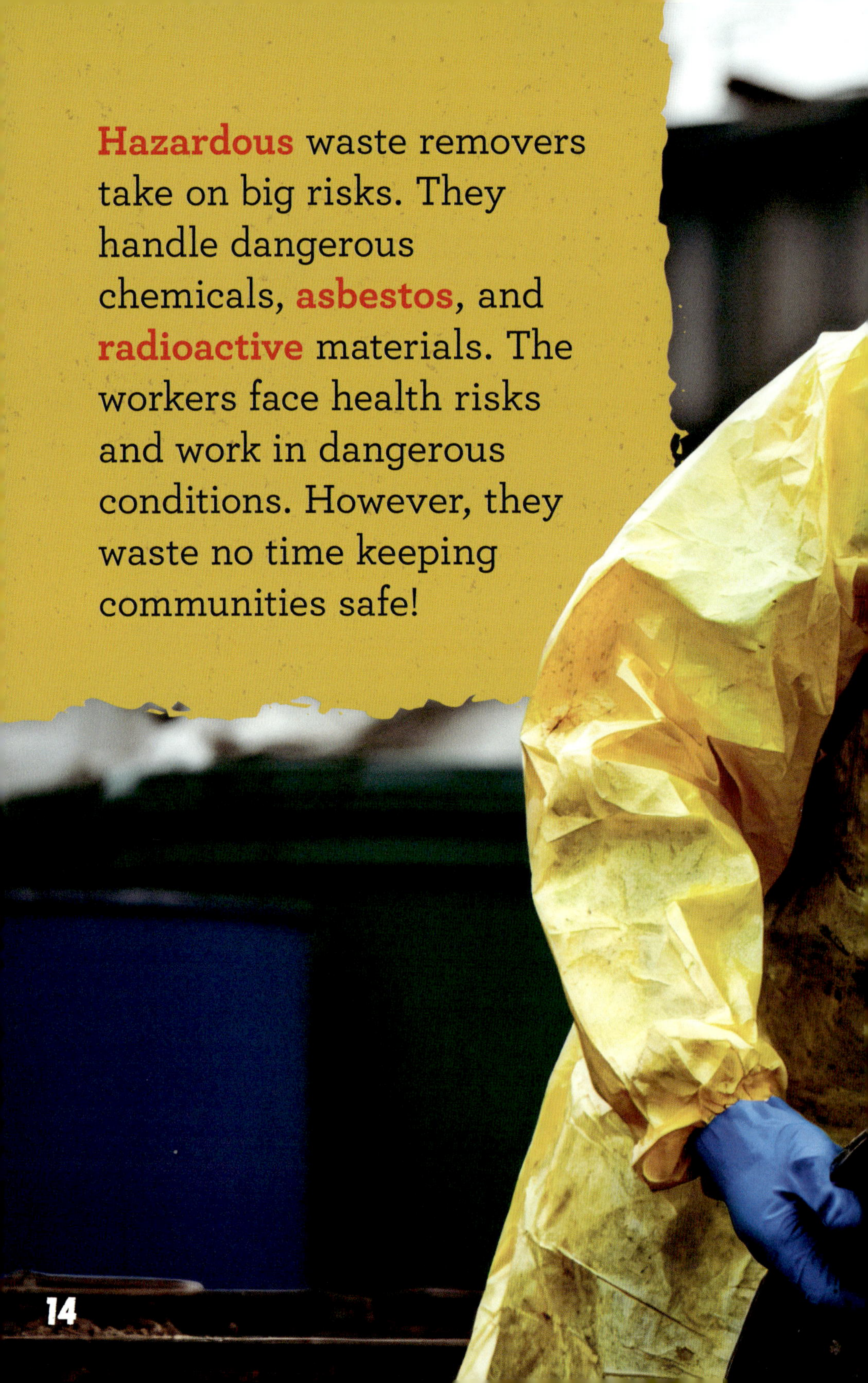

**Hazardous** waste removers take on big risks. They handle dangerous chemicals, **asbestos**, and **radioactive** materials. The workers face health risks and work in dangerous conditions. However, they waste no time keeping communities safe!

MOTORWAY
NX08 BZE
ROBINSONS
TRUCK BODIES
0191 4147744

Sometimes, portable toilets are the only option. Porta-potty servicers empty human waste from holding tanks. They keep everything clean and smelling as fresh as possible!

SLOW DOWN
New York City Bus
25DT-039
QW5
HE-5000
DON'T
LITTER

Garbage collectors gather up all waste from homes and businesses. Their job is physically demanding and involves smelly and **hazardous** materials. As if that weren't enough, garbage collectors have to watch out for broken glass!

Working on an oil rig is a dirty and dangerous job. Rig workers are exposed to harsh weather, unsafe chemicals, and dangerous heights. Known as black gold, the oil can be rather **crude**!

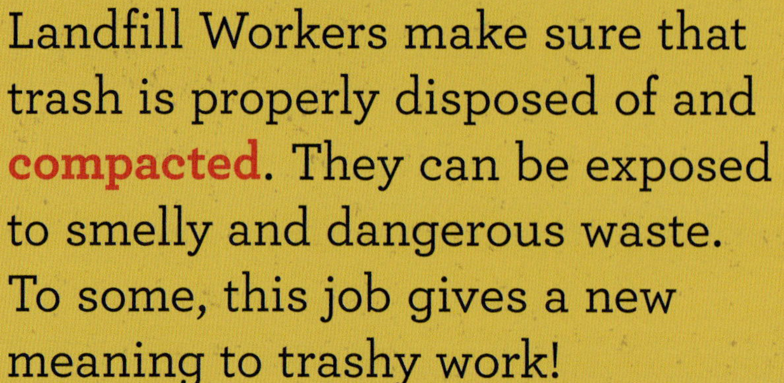

Landfill Workers make sure that trash is properly disposed of and **compacted**. They can be exposed to smelly and dangerous waste. To some, this job gives a new meaning to trashy work!

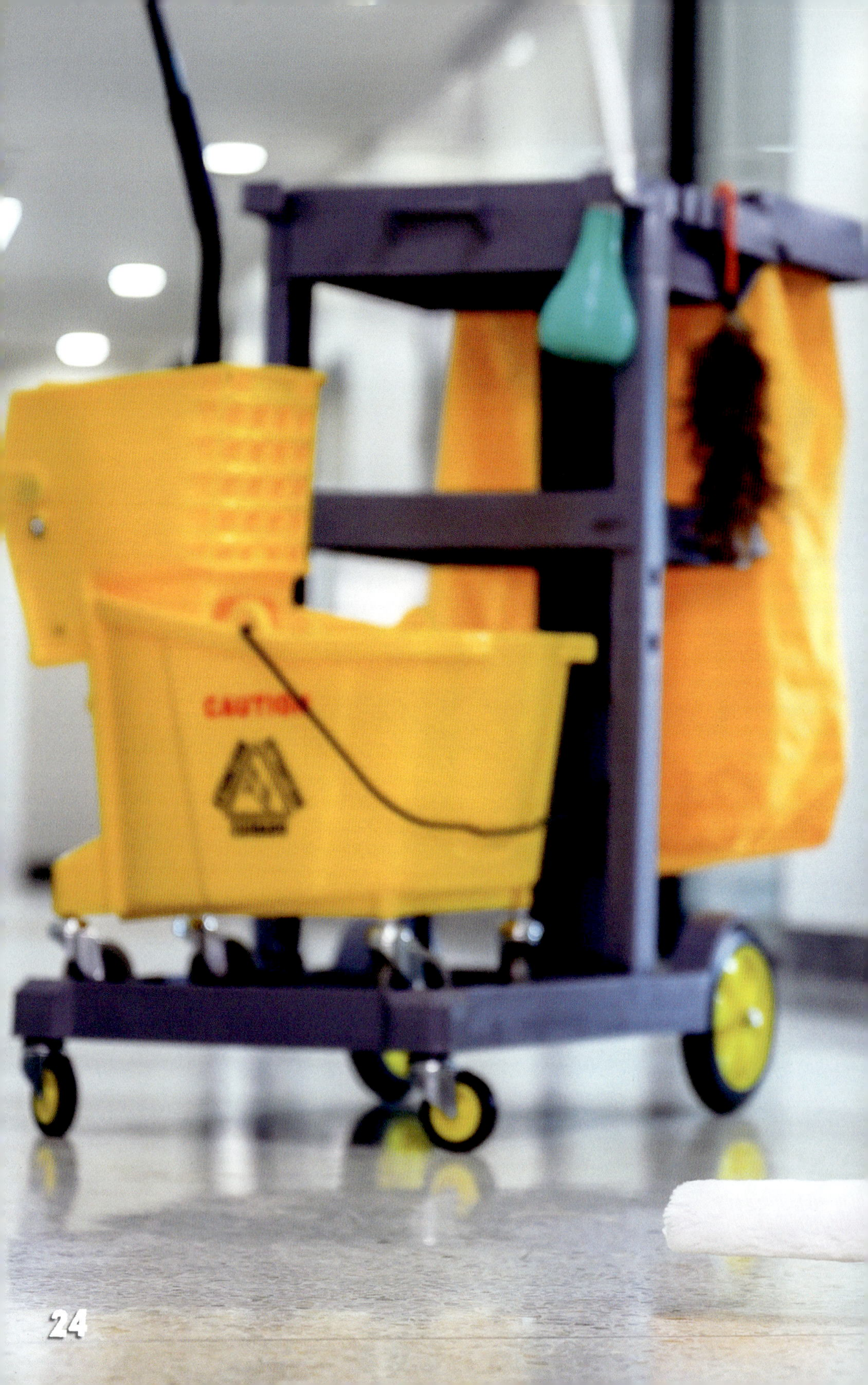

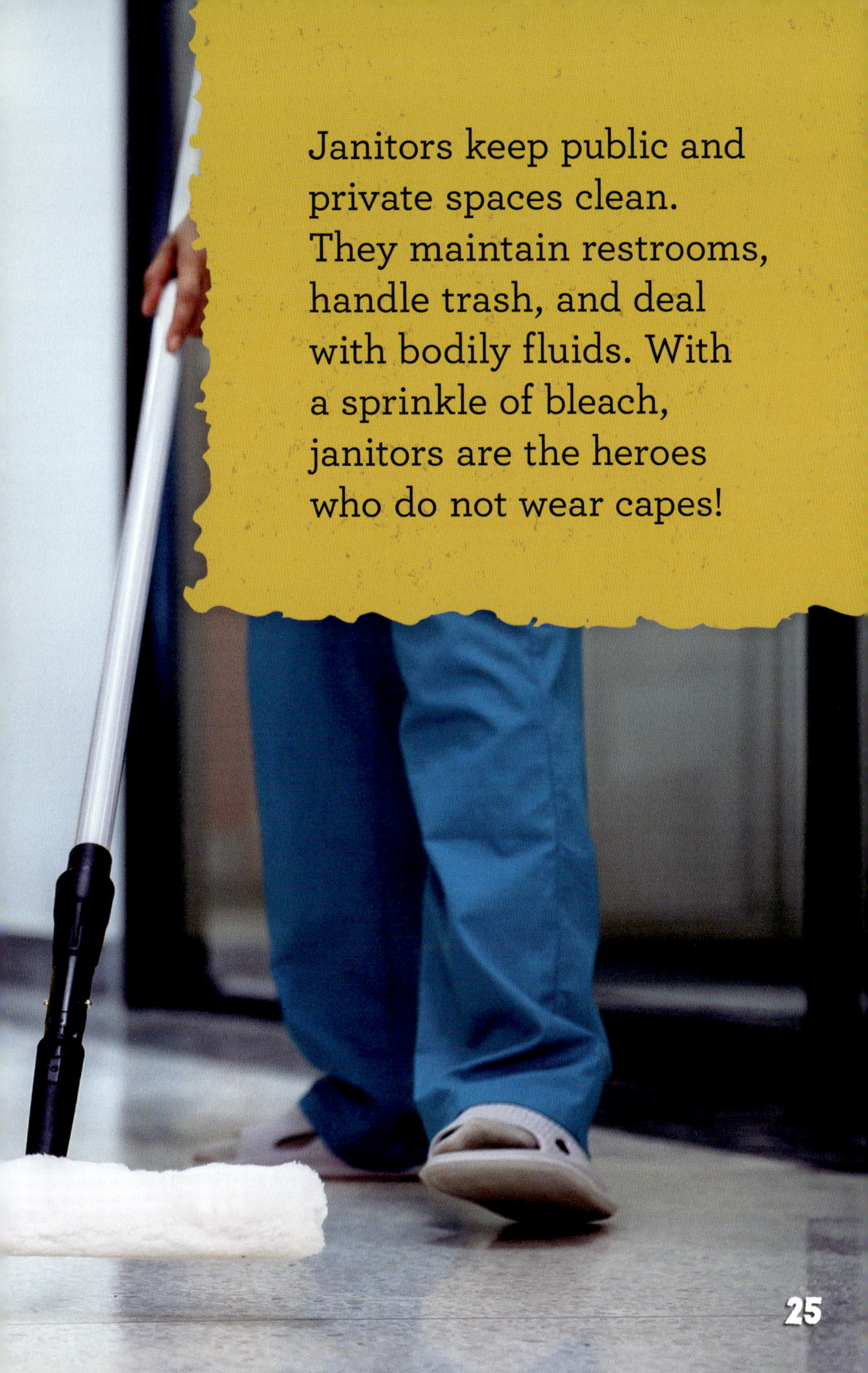

Janitors keep public and private spaces clean. They maintain restrooms, handle trash, and deal with bodily fluids. With a sprinkle of bleach, janitors are the heroes who do not wear capes!

# THE CLEAN UP

Community workers help strengthen the neighborhoods, towns, and cities where they work. While some of the work is dirty, all of it is important.

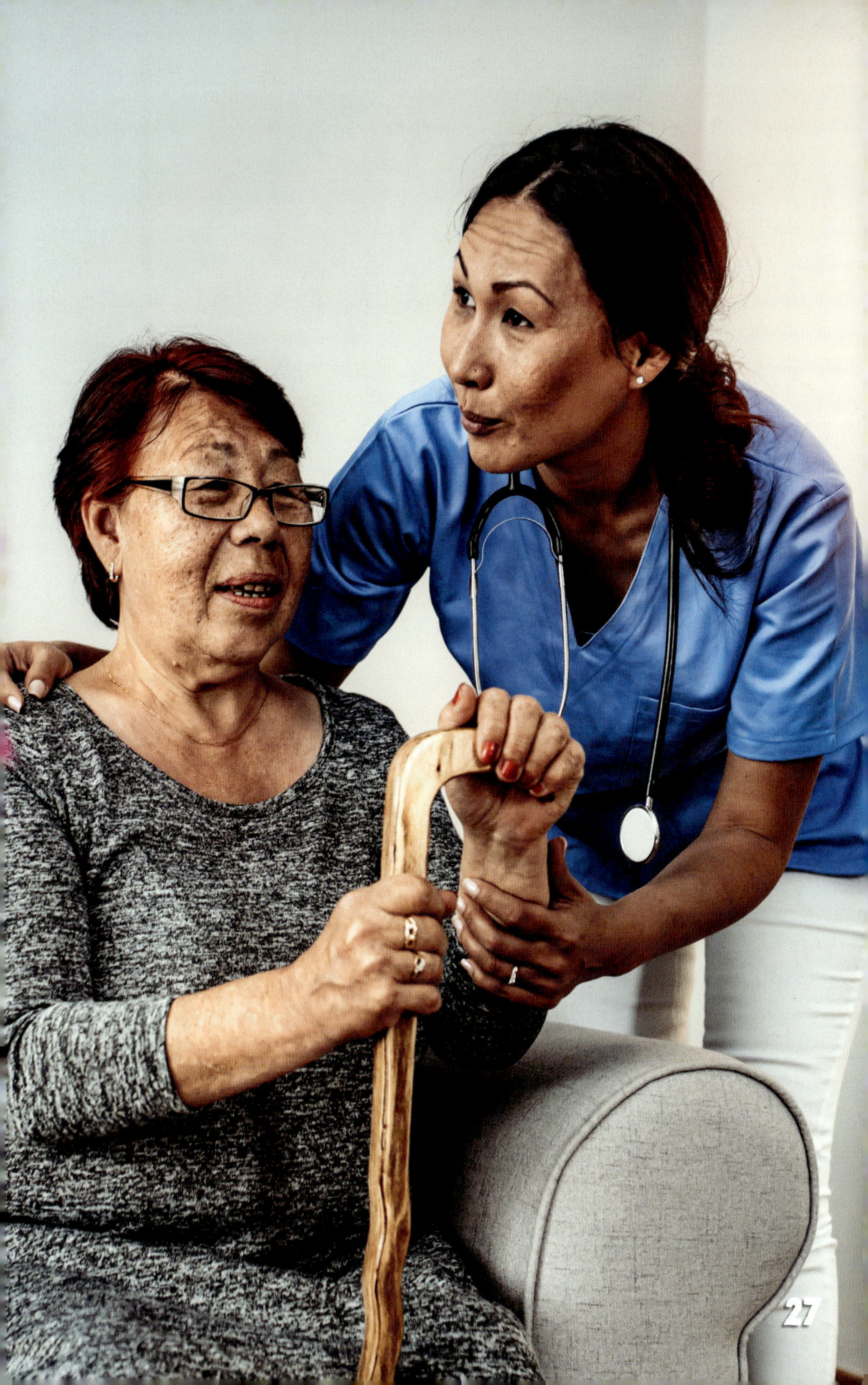

Dirty community jobs are considered the glue that holds society together. And it's not just because the work involves sticky situations!

# GLOSSARY

**asbestos** – a natural mineral that was used in buildings because it was fire-resistant. Its use stopped after it made people sick when inhaled.

**compact** – firmly packed together.

**crude** – natural or raw; offensive.

**grease trap** – a special container that traps grease and oil from sink water, preventing clogs and keeping the plumbing clean.

**hazardous** – full of danger or having many risks.

**radioactive** – material that releases harmful radiation that can cause illnesses such as cancers, and negatively impacts plants, animals, and the environment.

**raw** – being in or nearly in the natural state.

**sewage treatment** – cleaning dirty water from homes and businesses to make it safe for plants, animals, and people.

**welfare** – a state of health and happiness.

# ONLINE RESOURCES

Booklinks
NONFICTION NETWORK
FREE! ONLINE NONFICTION RESOURCES

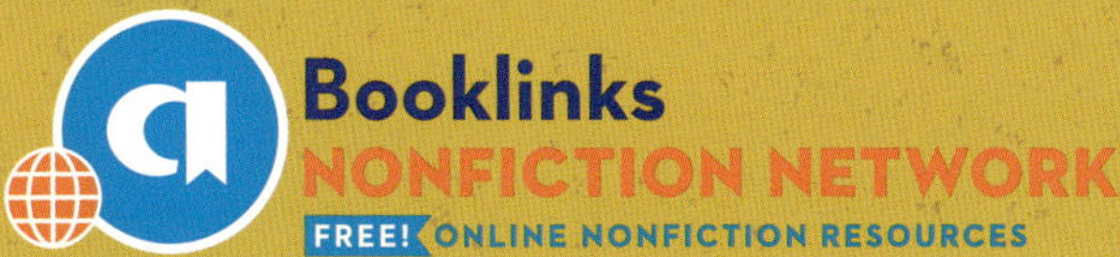

To learn more about dirty community jobs, please visit **abdobooklinks.com** or scan this QR code. These links are routinely monitored and updated to provide the most current information available.

# INDEX